The Step-By-Step Guide To The
VLOOKUP
formula in Microsoft® Excel®

C.J. Benton

DEDICATION

To users searching for a concise
Microsoft® Excel® VLOOKUP book!

CONTENTS

i

PREFACE

For nearly twenty years, I worked as a Data & Systems Analyst for three different Fortune 500 companies, primarily in the areas of Finance, Infrastructure Services, and Logistics. During that time I used Microsoft® Excel® extensively developing hundreds of different types of reports, analysis tools, and several forms of Dashboards.

I've utilized many Microsoft® Excel® features, including VLOOKUPS. The following are the VLOOKUP functions I used and taught the most to fellow colleagues.

CHAPTER 1
HOW TO USE THIS BOOK

This book can be used as a tutorial or quick reference guide. It is intended for users who are comfortable with the basics of Microsoft® Excel® and want to build upon this skill by learning the very useful VLOOKUP functionality.

This book assumes you already know how to create, open, save, and modify an Excel® workbook and have a general familiarity with the Excel® toolbar.

All of the examples in this book use Microsoft® Excel® 2013, however most of the functionality and formulas can be applied with Microsoft® Excel® version 2007 or later.

Please always **back-up your work** and **save often**. A good best practice when attempting any new functionality is to **create a copy of the original spreadsheet** and implement your changes on the copied spreadsheet. Should anything go wrong, you then have the original spreadsheet to fall back on. Please see the diagram below.

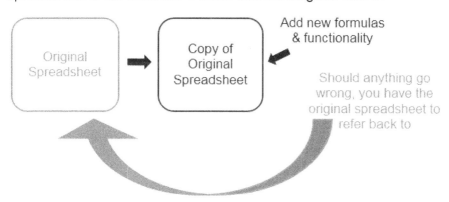

This book is structured to build on each previous chapter's teaching. Chapters 2, 3, & 4 cover the basic and intermediate features of VLOOKUP formulas. Chapter 5 goes into detail on how to apply the VLOOKUP formula across multiple workbooks and tabs. The final chapter examines some of the more common VLOOKUP error messages and how to resolve them.

The below table is a summary of the functionality and features detailed in each chapter:

CHAPTER	FUNCTIONALITY / FEATURE(S)
Chapter 2 VLOOKUP Basics	• What the VLOOKUP formula does • The parts of a VLOOKUP formula • Two detailed examples with screenshots using a basic VLOOKUP formula
Chapters 3 & 4 Taking VLOOKUPS to the next level	• Incorporating the IFERROR functionality into your VLOOKUP formula • What to do when you attempt to lookup a value in the table_array, but none exists • What to do when you don't have a unique lookup_value • What to do when the unique lookup_value is listed more than once in the table_array
Chapter 5 Using the VLOOKUP across tabs & workbooks	• Detailed example with screenshots of how to apply the VLOOKUP formula across multiple workbooks and tabs
Chapter 6 VLOOKUP Troubleshooting	• A review of five common VLOOKUP error messages / issues and how to resolve them

To enhance readability and for those who want to skip to specific areas, each chapter consists of _one or more_ of the following sections:

Diagram 2:

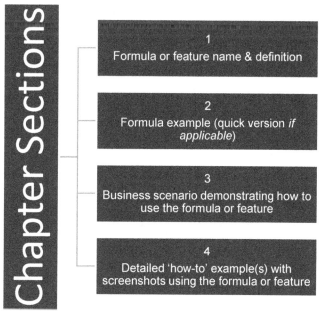

SECTION 1:

Provides the formula or feature name and definition for that chapter.

SECTION 2:

Gives a quick example of how to use the formula and the results. This is intended for intermediate level users who do not require a detailed step-by-step example. Also, this section can be used as a quick reference of the syntax.

SECTION 3:

Offers one or more business scenarios demonstrating how the formula or feature may be used.

SECTION 4:

Presents detailed instructions with screenshots explaining how to answer each chapter's scenario questions or how to resolve common error messages.

CHAPTER 2
INTRODUCTION TO THE VLOOKUP FORMULA

Formula:
- VLOOKUP

Definition:
- The VLOOKUP formula allows you to search for and return a value from another Excel® list to a new Excel® list based on a matching lookup value.

Quick Example:

```
Formula Syntax:

VLOOKUP (lookup_value, table_array, col_index_num,
[range_lookup])

All parameters are required, except for
[range_lookup]
```

	A	B	C	D
1	SALES PERSON ID	SALES	VLOOKUP FORMULA	RESULT
2	200	469	=VLOOKUP(A2,Sheet2!A2:B6,2,FALSE)	Graham, Peter

The VLOOKUP formula is made-up of four parts:

❶ lookup value:

This is the field you want to find (match) typically located on another tab or spreadsheet.

In the example below, **'A2'** is selected which has the Sales Person ID value of **'200'**. I will look to match this value on the tab labeled **'Sheet2'**. Sales Person Name is the value I want to look-up and be returned to the tab labeled **'Sheet1'**.

❷ table array:

This is the spreadsheet (tab) and range of cells that are searched for the ❶ lookup_value. The field you want to match <u>must be</u> in the <u>first column</u> of the range of cells you specify in the ❷ table_array.

In the example below, I'm searching the tab labeled **'Sheet2'** with the cell range of **'A2:B6'**.

❸ col index num:

Is the column that contains the value you want returned.

In the example below, column **'2'** of the tab labeled **'Sheet2'** contains value of Sales Person Name that I want returned to the tab labeled **'Sheet1'**.

❹ range lookup:

Is the optional value of **'TRUE'** or **'FALSE'**. The value of **'FALSE'** will return an *exact* match, while **'TRUE'** will return an *approximate* match. Most users enter **'FALSE'** for this parameter.

Below, I have entered **'FALSE'** for an exact match.

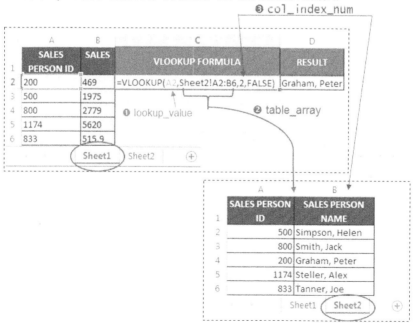

Scenario:
You've been asked to provide a list of the first quarter sales by month, for each sales person. You run a query from the sales database and generate an Excel® report. Unfortunately, the database only contains the sales person's ID, but not their name. You use a VLOOKUP formula to pull the Sales Person's Name from an existing Excel® spreadsheet to the new sales report.

Detailed Example How To Use The Formula:
To download a free copy of the Excel® file used in this scenario please go to:
http://bentonexcelbooks.my-free.website/sample-data-files select the file for *Chapter 2 (VLOOKUP) in the 'The Step-By-Step Guide To The* *VLOOKUP formula in Microsoft® Excel®' section.*
  Sample data (Sales Report with ID only):

	A	B	C	D
1	**SALES PERSON ID**	**Jan**	**Feb**	**Mar**
2	200	$ 869	$ 1,092	$ 1,550
3	500	$ 1,975	$ 2,274	$ 2,719
4	800	$ 2,779	$ 3,002	$ 3,460
5	833	$ 7,716	$ 8,015	$ 8,460
6	1174	$ 5,620	$ 5,843	$ 6,301

Sheet1 Sheet2

  Sample data (Sales Person Name):

	A	B
1	**SALES PERSON ID**	**SALES PERSON NAME**
2	800	Smith, Jack
3	200	Graham, Peter
4	1174	Steller, Alex
5	500	Simpson, Helen
6	833	Tanner, Joe

Sheet1 Sheet2

1. On **'Sheet1'**, Insert a new column between columns **'A'** & **'B,'** label it "**SALES PERSON NAME**"

2. Next, apply the **'VLOOKUP'** formula for 'Sales Person Name' by clicking in cell '**B2**'

	A	B	C	D	E
	SALES PERSON ID	**SALES PERSON NAME**	**Jan**	**Feb**	**Mar**
1					
2	200		$ 869	$ 1,092	$ 1,550
3	500		$ 1,975	$ 2,274	$ 2,719
4	800		$ 2,779	$ 3,002	$ 3,460
5	833		$ 7,716	$ 8,015	$ 8,460
6	1174		$ 5,620	$ 5,843	$ 6,301

3. From the toolbar select **Formulas : Insert Function**

4. Type "**VLOOKUP**" in the **'Search for a function:'** dialogue box

5. Click the '**Go**' button

The following dialogue box should now appear:

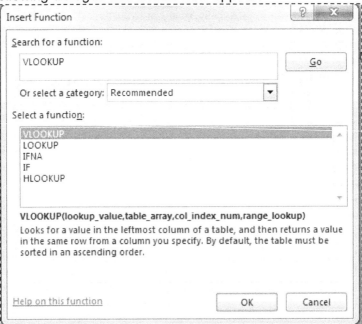

6. Click the '**OK**' button

7. Click cell '**A2**' or enter **A2** in the dialogue box for the '**Lookup_value**' *(the sales person ID is the field we'll lookup on '*Sheet2*')*

8. For '**Table_array**', click on the tab '**Sheet2**' and highlight cells '**A2:B6**' *(this is the range of cells we're searching)*

9. Enter the number **2** for '**Col_index_num**' *(this is the column with the sales person's name)*

10. For '**Range_lookup**' enter **FALSE**

11. Click the '**OK**' button

The following should be the result:

B2	▼	⋮	×	✓	*fx*	=VLOOKUP(A2,Sheet2!A2:B6,2,FALSE)

	A	B	C	D	E	F
1	SALES PERSON ID	SALES PERSON NAME	Jan	Feb	Mar	
2	200	Graham, Peter	$ 869	$ 1,092	$ 1,550	
3	500		$ 1,975	$ 2,274	$ 2,719	
4	800		$ 2,779	$ 3,002	$ 3,460	
5	833		$ 7,716	$ 8,015	$ 8,460	
6	1174		$ 5,620	$ 5,843	$ 6,301	

12. We need to do one additional step before we can copy this formula down to cells '**B3**' thru '**B6**.' We must add the dollar symbol **$** to the '**Table_array**'. This will prevent our cell range from changing:

=VLOOKUP(A2,Sheet2!$A$2:$B$6,2,FALSE)

If we attempted to copy the VLOOKUP formula to cells '**B3**' thru '**B6**,' without adding the **$**, the result would be as follows, **_NOTE:_** *how the* '*Table_array*' *cell range changes:*

	A	B
1	SALES PERSON ID	SALES PERSON NAME
2	200	=VLOOKUP(A2,Sheet2!$A$2:$B$6,2,FALSE)
3	500	=VLOOKUP(A3,Sheet2!A3:B7,2,FALSE)
4	800	=VLOOKUP(A4,Sheet2!A4:B8,2,FALSE)
5	833	=VLOOKUP(A5,Sheet2!A5:B9,2,FALSE)
6	1174	=VLOOKUP(A6,Sheet2!A6:B10,2,FALSE)

We would also receive an error in cells '**B4**' & '**B6**'

	A	B	C	D	E
1	SALES PERS	SALES PERSON NAME	Jan	Feb	Mar
2	200	Graham, Peter	$ 869	$ 1,092	$ 1,550
3	500	Simpson, Helen	$ 1,975	$ 2,274	$ 2,719
4	800	#N/A	$ 2,779	$ 3,002	$ 3,460
5	833	Tanner, Joe	$ 7,716	$ 8,015	$ 8,460
6	1174	#N/A	$ 5,620	$ 5,843	$ 6,301

13. After adding the $ to the 'Table_array', copy the VLOOKUP formula to cells 'B3' thru 'B6'

We have successfully looked-up and added the Sales Person Name to the quarterly sales report. We can now provide a list of the first quarter sales by month, for each sales person.

	A	B	C	D	E
1	SALES PERS	SALES PERSON NAME	Jan	Feb	Mar
2	200	Graham, Peter	$ 869	$ 1,092	$ 1,550
3	500	Simpson, Helen	$ 1,975	$ 2,274	$ 2,719
4	800	Smith, Jack	$ 2,779	$ 3,002	$ 3,460
5	833	Tanner, Joe	$ 7,716	$ 8,015	$ 8,460
6	1174	Steller, Alex	$ 5,620	$ 5,843	$ 6,301

Alternatively, for the 'Table_array' you may enter the columns A:B (Sheet2!A:B) instead of the range of cells (Sheet2!$A$2:$B$6), if the *entire column* contains the data you want returned, this would eliminate the need to complete **step 12**.

Let's walk through another example, this time using columns for the 'Table_array' instead of the range of cells. In this example, I will also demonstrate another option to enter the VLOOKUP formula.

Scenario:

You've now been asked to include the **sales region** to the list of the first quarter sales by month, for each sales person.

Detailed Example How To Use The Formula:

*Sample data (Sales Report with ID & **Name**):*

	A	B	C	D	E
1	SALES PERS	SALES PERSON NAME	Jan	Feb	Mar
2	200	Graham, Peter	$ 869	$ 1,092	$ 1,550
3	500	Simpson, Helen	$ 1,975	$ 2,274	$ 2,719
4	800	Smith, Jack	$ 2,779	$ 3,002	$ 3,460
5	833	Tanner, Joe	$ 7,716	$ 8,015	$ 8,460
6	1174	Steller, Alex	$ 5,620	$ 5,843	$ 6,301

Sheet1　Sheet2　⊕

*Sample data (Sales Person Name & **Region**):*

	A	B	C
1	SALES PERSON ID	SALES PERSON NAME	REGION
2	800	Smith, Jack	East
3	200	Graham, Peter	West
4	1174	Steller, Alex	Central
5	500	Simpson, Helen	East
6	833	Tanner, Joe	West

Sheet1　Sheet2　⊕

1. On **'Sheet1'**, Insert a new column between columns **'B'** & **'C,'** label it "**REGION**"

2. Next, apply the '**VLOOKUP**' formula for 'REGION' by clicking in cell 'C2'

	A	B	C	D	E	F
1	SALES PERS	SALES PERSON NAME	REGION	Jan	Feb	Mar
2	200	Graham, Peter		$ 869	$ 1,092	$ 1,550
3	500	Simpson, Helen		$ 1,975	$ 2,274	$ 2,719
4	800	Smith, Jack		$ 2,779	$ 3,002	$ 3,460
5	833	Tanner, Joe		$ 7,716	$ 8,015	$ 8,460
6	1174	Steller, Alex		$ 5,620	$ 5,843	$ 6,301

3. From the toolbar select **Formulas**
4. Click the drop-down box for **Lookup & Reference**
5. Select **VLOOKUP**

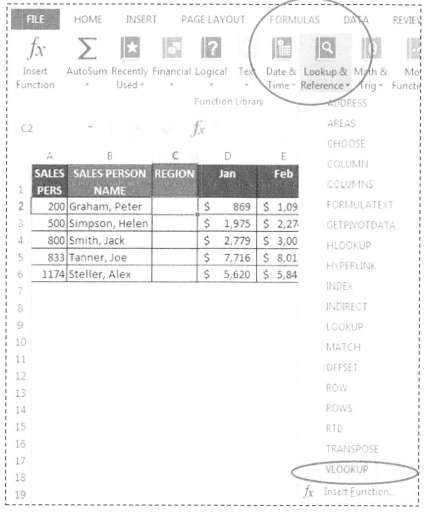

6. Click cell '**A2**' or enter **A2** in the dialogue box for the '**Lookup_value**' *(the sales person ID is the field we'll lookup on '**Sheet2**')*

7. For '**Table_array**', click on the tab '**Sheet2**' and highlight columns '**A:C**' *(this is the range of cells we're searching)*

8. Enter the number **3** for '**Col_index_num**' *(this is the column with the sales person's region)*

9. For '**Range_lookup**' enter **FALSE**

10. Click the '**OK**' button

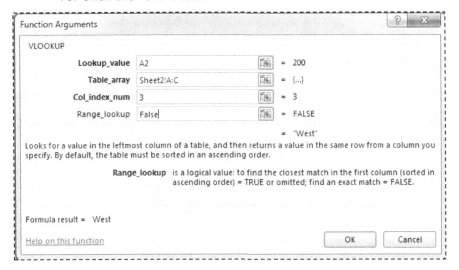

The following should be the result:

	A	B	C	D	E	F	G
	SALES PERS	**SALES PERSON NAME**	**REGION**	**Jan**	**Feb**	**Mar**	
1							
2	200	Graham, Peter	West	$ 869	$ 1,092	$ 1,550	
3	500	Simpson, Helen		$ 1,975	$ 2,274	$ 2,719	
4	800	Smith, Jack		$ 2,779	$ 3,002	$ 3,460	
5	833	Tanner, Joe		$ 7,716	$ 8,015	$ 8,460	
6	1174	Steller, Alex		$ 5,620	$ 5,843	$ 6,301	

C2 — fx =VLOOKUP(A2,Sheet2!A:C,3,FALSE)

11. Copy this formula down to cells '**C3**' thru '**C6**'

The following should be the result:

	A	B	C	D	E	F
	SALES PERS	SALES PERSON NAME	REGION	Jan	Feb	Mar
1						
2	200	Graham, Peter	West	$ 869	$ 1,092	$ 1,550
3	500	Simpson, Helen	East	$ 1,975	$ 2,274	$ 2,719
4	800	Smith, Jack	East	$ 2,779	$ 3,002	$ 3,460
5	833	Tanner, Joe	West	$ 7,716	$ 8,015	$ 8,460
6	1174	Steller, Alex	Central	$ 5,620	$ 5,843	$ 6,301

We have successfully looked-up and added the Sales Person's **Region** to the quarterly sales report.

☑ HELPFUL INFORMATION:

When sending the results of a VLOOKUP to a customer or a co-worker, a common mistake beginners often make is including the VLOOKUP formula in the spreadsheet, rather than pasting the results as a value. This is a very easy thing to do, but depending on where the **Table_array** sheet or workbook is located can cause the following to happen.

1. Let's say in the example above, after adding the Sales Person Name & Region you deleted, '**Sheet2**', because you no longer needed it.

   a. You saved the workbook without noticing the VLOOKUP formula is now broken.

b. You emailed the spreadsheet results to the customer.

c. When they open the spreadsheet, they likely would see an error in the results:

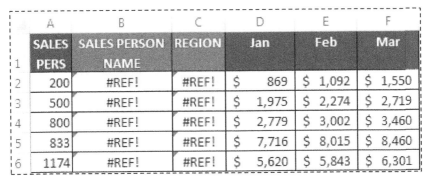

	A	B	C	D	E	F
1	SALES PERS	SALES PERSON NAME	REGION	Jan	Feb	Mar
2	200	#REF!	#REF!	$ 869	$ 1,092	$ 1,550
3	500	#REF!	#REF!	$ 1,975	$ 2,274	$ 2,719
4	800	#REF!	#REF!	$ 2,779	$ 3,002	$ 3,460
5	833	#REF!	#REF!	$ 7,716	$ 8,015	$ 8,460
6	1174	#REF!	#REF!	$ 5,620	$ 5,843	$ 6,301

2. Another common scenario, if the **Table_array** was located in a separate workbook.

a. You saved the workbook without issue.

b. You emailed the spreadsheet results to a co-worker.

c. When they open the spreadsheet, they likely would see a **!SECURITY WARING** message about the file being linked to another workbook:

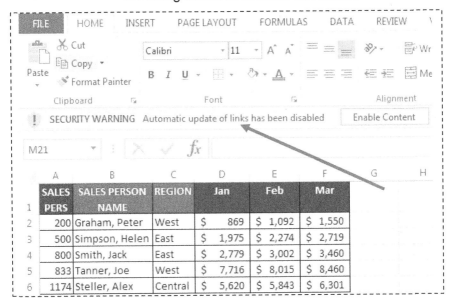

    d. If they clicked the **'Enable Content'** button, they may receive the following message:

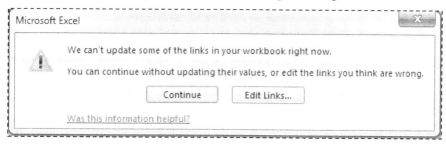

In either scenario, it could cause confusion, rework, or even lead the customer to have questions about you or the company / department you represent.

One of the easiest ways to address this issue is to **simply paste your VLOOKUP results as a value**. In the example above, we would:

1. Highlight cells '**B2**' thru '**C6**'
2. Click the '**Copy**' button or **CTL+C** from your keyboard
3. **Right click** and from the menu select **'Paste Special...'**
4. Select the '**Values**' radio button
5. Click the '**OK**' button

Please see screenshot below for an example:

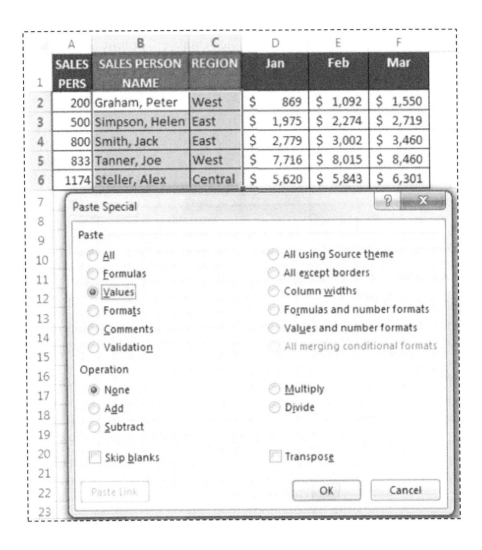

The VLOOKUP results are intact without any risk of error when you send them to a customer or a co-worker.

CHAPTER 3
FORMULAS = IF & NESTED IF STATEMENTS

Before extending the VLOOKUP functionality, we must **quickly** review IF & NESTED IF formulas. If you're already familiar with these logic functions, please skip and go to chapter 4.

Formula:
- IF

Definition:
- IF formulas allow you test conditions and return one value *if true* and another *if false*.

- NESTED IF formula allows you test conditions and return one value *if true* and another *if false*, if certain criteria is met.

Quick Example:

```
Formula Syntax:

IF(logical_test, value_if_true, [value_if_false])

logic_test required, value_if_true required,
value_if_false optional
```

Basic IF formula:

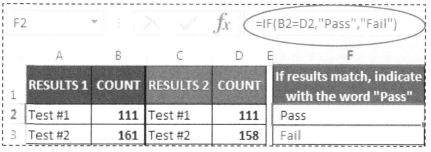

	A	B	C	D	E	F
	F2				f_x	=IF(B2=D2,"Pass","Fail")
1	RESULTS 1	COUNT	RESULTS 2	COUNT		If results match, indicate with the word "Pass"
2	Test #1	111	Test #1	111		Pass
3	Test #2	161	Test #2	158		Fail

Nested IF formula:

F4	▼ : ✕ ✓ f_x	=IF(B4=D4,"Pass",IF(B4-D4>5,"BIG FAIL","Fail"))

	A	B	C	D	E	F
1	RESULTS 1	COUNT	RESULTS 2	COUNT		IF results match = **Pass** IF results DO NOT match = **Fail** IF results DO NOT match and the difference is greater than 5 = **BIG FAIL**
2	Test #1	111	Test #1	111		Pass
3	Test #2	161	Test #2	158		Fail
4	Test #3	183	Test #3	175		BIG FAIL
5	Test #4	243	Test #4	243		Pass
6	Test #5	263	Test #5	260		Fail

If you would like to learn more about **IF** & **NESTED** formulas, please check out my book:

The Step-By-Step Guide To

The 25 Most Common Microsoft Excel Formulas & Features

CHAPTER 4
ENHANCED VLOOKUP FORMULAS

In this chapter we will extend the VLOOKUP functionality and examine some challenges that arise when using the VLOOKUP formula such as:

1. What to do when you attempt to lookup a value in the **table_array**, but none exists

2. What to do when you don't have a unique **lookup_value**

3. When the unique **lookup_value** is listed more than once in the **table_array**

This chapter also introduces two new formulas **IFERROR** and **CONCATENATE**. Let's begin with the IFERROR function.

Formula:
- IFERROR

Definition:
- IFERROR returns a value you specify if *(in our case the VLOOKUP)* formula evaluates an error such as: #N/A, #VALUE!, #REF!, #DIV/0!, #NUM!, #NAME?, or #NULL! Otherwise IFERROR will return the result of the *(VLOOKUP)* formula.

Quick Example:

```
Formula Syntax:
IFERROR(value, value_if_error)
All parameters are required
```

| | B4 | | | ▼ | : | ⤬ | ✓ | *fx* | =IFERROR(VLOOKUP(A4,Sheet2!A:C,2,FALSE),"Name Not Found") |

	A	B	C	D	E	F	G	H	I
1	SALES PERS	SALES PERSON NAME	REGION	Jan	Feb	Mar			
2	200	Graham, Peter	West	$ 869	$ 1,092	$ 1,550			
3	500	Simpson, Helen	East	$ 1,975	$ 2,274	$ 2,719			
4	800	Name Not Found	#N/A	$ 2,779	$ 3,002	$ 3,460			
5	833	Tanner, Joe	West	$ 7,716	$ 8,015	$ 8,460			
6	1174	Steller, Alex	Central	$ 5,620	$ 5,843	$ 6,301			

Scenario:

You've been asked to provide a list of the first quarter sales by month, for each sales person. However, *if* the Sales Person's name is not available, display the text **"Name Not Found."** You use a combination formula of IFERROR & VLOOKUP to develop this sales report.

Detailed Example How To Use The Formula:

To download a free copy of the Excel® file used in this scenario please go to:
http://bentonexcelbooks.my-free.website/sample-data-files select the file for Chapter 4 (IFERROR) in the 'The Step-By-Step Guide To The VLOOKUP formula in Microsoft® Excel®' section

Sample data (Sales Report with ID only):

	A	B	C	D	E
1	SALES PERS	SALES PERSON NAME	Jan	Feb	Mar
2	200		$ 869	$ 1,092	$ 1,550
3	500		$ 1,975	$ 2,274	$ 2,719
4	800		$ 2,779	$ 3,002	$ 3,460
5	833		$ 7,716	$ 8,015	$ 8,460
6	1174		$ 5,620	$ 5,843	$ 6,301

Sheet1 | Sheet2 ⊕

Sample data (Sales Person Name):

	A	B	C
1	SALES PERSON ID	SALES PERSON NAME	REGION
2	200	Graham, Peter	West
3	1174	Steller, Alex	Central
4	500	Simpson, Helen	East
5	833	Tanner, Joe	West

Sheet1 (Sheet2) ⊕

1. Select cell **'B2'** on **'Sheet1'**

2. Add the **VLOOKUP** formula:

   `=VLOOKUP(A2,Sheet2!A:C,2,FALSE)`

The following should be the result:

B2   ▼   :   ✕   ✓   *fx*   =VLOOKUP(A2,Sheet2!A:C,2,FALSE)

	A	B	C	D	E	F
1	SALES PERS	SALES PERSON NAME	Jan	Feb	Mar	
2	200	Graham, Peter	$ 869	$ 1,092	$ 1,550	
3	500		$ 1,975	$ 2,274	$ 2,719	
4	800		$ 2,779	$ 3,002	$ 3,460	
5	833		$ 7,716	$ 8,015	$ 8,460	
6	1174		$ 5,620	$ 5,843	$ 6,301	

3. Copy this formula down to cells **'B3'** thru **'B6'**

Note: the error **#N/A** in cell **'B4'**, this is because on the **table_array (Sheet2)** there is no Sales Person ID for ID# 800

	A	B	C	D	E
1	**SALES PERSON ID**	**SALES PERSON NAME**	**Jan**	**Feb**	**Mar**
2	200	Graham, Peter	$ 869	$ 1,092	$ 1,550
3	500	Simpson, Helen	$ 1,975	$ 2,274	$ 2,719
4	800	#N/A	$ 2,779	$ 3,002	$ 3,460
5	833	Tanner, Joe	$ 7,716	$ 8,015	$ 8,460
6	1174	Steller, Alex	$ 5,620	$ 5,843	$ 6,301

We were asked to provide a list of the first quarter sales by month, for each sales person. However, *if* the Sales Person's name is not available, display the text **"Name Not Found."** To address this requirement of *if the Sales Person's name is not found, display the* text *"Name Not Found"* we will add the function **IFERROR** to our **VLOOKUP** formula.

4. Select cell **'B2'** on **'Sheet1'**

5. Add the **IFERROR** formula to the existing **VLOOKUP** function:

```
=IFERROR(VLOOKUP(A2,Sheet2!A:C,2,FALSE),"Name Not Found")
```

The following should be the result:

B2			f_x	=IFERROR(VLOOKUP(A2,Sheet2!A:C,2,FALSE),"Name Not Found")

	A	B	C	D	E	F	G	H	I
1	**SALES PERSON ID**	**SALES PERSON NAME**	**Jan**	**Feb**	**Mar**				
2	200	Graham, Peter	$ 869	$ 1,092	$ 1,550				
3	500	Simpson, Helen	$ 1,975	$ 2,274	$ 2,719				
4	800	#N/A	$ 2,779	$ 3,002	$ 3,460				
5	833	Tanner, Joe	$ 7,716	$ 8,015	$ 8,460				
6	1174	Steller, Alex	$ 5,620	$ 5,843	$ 6,301				

6. Copy this formula down to cells '**B3**' thru '**B6**'

Note: the previous error of **#N/A** in cell '**B4**' is gone and now displays "Name Not Found"

	A	B	C	D	E
1	SALES PERSON ID	SALES PERSON NAME	Jan	Feb	Mar
2	200	Graham, Peter	$ 869	$ 1,092	$ 1,550
3	500	Simpson, Helen	$ 1,975	$ 2,274	$ 2,719
4	800	Name Not Found	$ 2,779	$ 3,002	$ 3,460
5	833	Tanner, Joe	$ 7,716	$ 8,015	$ 8,460
6	1174	Steller, Alex	$ 5,620	$ 5,843	$ 6,301

You've now created a list of the first quarter sales by month, for each sales person and when the Sales Person's name is not available, the text **"Name Not Found"** is displayed.

☑ HELPFUL INFORMATION:

The **IF**ERROR formula was introduced in Microsoft® Excel® version 2007, prior to this, many of us would use **IS**ERROR. I include an example of **IS**ERROR in this book, because I still see many people use this formula in spreadsheets today. In the exercise above, someone may use the **IS**ERROR formula to accomplish the same thing as **IF**ERROR, below is an example of the how the formula would be written:

```
=IF(ISERROR(VLOOKUP(A2,Sheet2!A:C,2,FALSE)),"Name Not
Found",(VLOOKUP(A2,Sheet2!A:C,2,FALSE)))
```

	SALES PERSON ID	SALES PERSON NAME	Jan	Feb	Mar
1					
2	200	Graham, Peter	$ 869	$ 1,092	$ 1,550
3	500	Simpson, Helen	$ 1,975	$ 2,274	$ 2,719
4	800	Name Not Found	$ 2,779	$ 3,002	$ 3,460
5	833	Tanner, Joe	$ 7,716	$ 8,015	$ 8,460
6	1174	Steller, Alex	$ 5,620	$ 5,843	$ 6,301

B4 =IF(ISERROR(VLOOKUP(A4,Sheet2!A:C,2,FALSE)),"Name Not Found",(VLOOKUP(A4,Sheet2!A:C,2,FALSE)))

As you can see **IF**ERROR greatly simplifies this type of functionality.

Another common issue that arises when using the VLOOKUP formula is occasionally you will *not* have a unique **lookup_value**. In all of the previous examples, we used a unique sale person ID number. What would we do if all we had was a list of first and last names? To tackle this question, we're going to introduce another formula called **CONCATENATE**. If you're already familiar with concatenation, please skip this section and go to page 31.

Formula:
- CONCATENATE

Definition:
- **CONCATENATE:** Joins two or more cells together and also allows the option to insert additional text into the merged cell.

Quick Example:

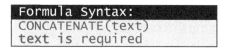

```
Formula Syntax:
CONCATENATE(text)
text is required
```

	A	B	C	D
	SALES PERSON FIRST NAME	**SALES PERSON LAST NAME**	**FORMULA**	Merged cells 'B2' & 'A2', Last Name, followed by a comma and space, then First Name
1				
2	Jack	Smith	=CONCATENATE(B2,", ",A2)	Smith, Jack

Scenario

You've been given a list of employees that need to be notified of a change in healthcare benefits. You've been asked to:

1. Generate an email list based on these names

Detailed Example How To Use The Formula:

Sample data:

	A	B
	EMPLOYEE FIRST NAME	**EMPLOYEE LAST NAME**
1		
2	Jack	Smith
3	Joe	Tanner
4	Peter	Graham
5	Helen	Simpson
6	Alex	Steller

1. Add a column, in cell **'C1'** label it "**EMAIL ADDRESS**"

2. Next, apply the '**CONCATENATION**' function for the Employee First & Last names to cell **'C2'**

	A	B	C
	EMPLOYEE FIRST NAME	**EMPLOYEE LAST NAME**	**EMAIL ADDRESS**
1			
2	Jack	Smith	
3	Joe	Tanner	
4	Peter	Graham	
5	Helen	Simpson	
6	Alex	Steller	

3. From the toolbar select **FORMULAS** and the **'Text'** drop-down box

4. Select **'CONCATENATE'**

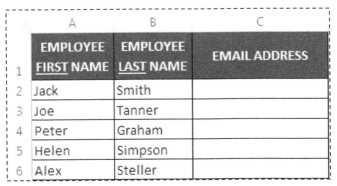

The following dialogue should now appear:

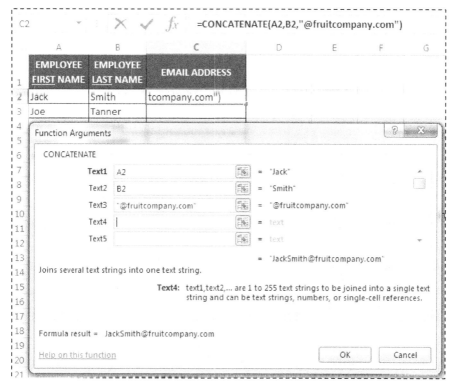

5. **Text1** box click cell '**A2**' or enter **A2**

6. **Text2** box click cell '**B2**' or enter **B2**

7. **Text3** box enter the text '**@fruitcompany.com**' *(you do not need to enter the quotation marks, these will be automatically added when using the formula wizard)*

8. Click the '**OK**' button

9. Copy the **CONCATENATE** formula down cells '**C3**' thru '**C6**'

C2	▾ : ✕ ✓ *fx*	=CONCATENATE(A2,B2,"@fruitcompany.com")

	A	B	C	D	E
1	EMPLOYEE FIRST NAME	EMPLOYEE LAST NAME	EMAIL ADDRESS		
2	Jack	Smith	JackSmith@fruitcompany.com		
3	Joe	Tanner	JoeTanner@fruitcompany.com		
4	Peter	Graham	PeterGraham@fruitcompany.com		
5	Helen	Simpson	HelenSimpson@fruitcompany.com		
6	Alex	Steller	AlexSteller@fruitcompany.com		

We now have an email list.

Alternatively, we can perform the same type of functionality WITHOUT using the formula wizard for CONCATENATE. Instead, we can use the **ampersand (&)** symbol. This is how most intermediate and advanced Excel® users typically execute this command. Please see below for an example:

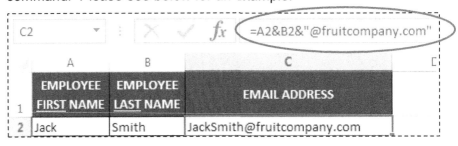

C2	▾ : ✕ ✓ *fx*	=A2&B2&"@fruitcompany.com"	

	A	B	C	D
1	EMPLOYEE FIRST NAME	EMPLOYEE LAST NAME	EMAIL ADDRESS	
2	Jack	Smith	JackSmith@fruitcompany.com	

Now that we've reviewed concatenation, let's take a look at how this formula can assist us when you don't have a unique **lookup_value**.

Scenario

You've been given a list of employees and their first quarter sales results and need to lookup what sales region each employee belongs too. You attempt to use the VLOOKUP formula, however upon further review of the two files, you see that the sales report contains only the sales person's first and last name, but not their sales person ID number. Therefore, you're not sure what the unique **lookup_value** should be. You're unable to lookup based on first or last name alone, because more than one employee has the either the same first or last name. You decide to use the CONCATENATE function to create a unique **lookup_value**.

Detailed Example How To Use The Formula:

Sample data (Sales Report with no Sales Person ID):

> *To download a free copy of the Excel® file used in this scenario please go to:*
> *http://bentonexcelbooks.my-free.website/sample-data-files*
> *select the file for Chapter 4 (Sales Report) in the 'The Step-By-Step Guide To The VLOOKUP formula in Microsoft® Excel®' section.*

	A	B	C	D	E
	SALES PERSON FIRST	SALES PERSON LAST	Jan	Feb	Mar
2	Peter	Danner	$ 4,449	$ 7,048	$ 5,746
3	Maggie	Graham	$ 3,973	$ 6,251	$ 7,719
4	Peter	Graham	$ 1,975	$ 2,274	$ 2,719
5	Helen	Simpson	$ 7,716	$ 8,015	$ 8,460
6	Alex	Steller	$ 2,779	$ 3,002	$ 3,460
7	Joe	Tanner	$ 5,620	$ 5,843	$ 6,301
8	Elizabeth	Winchester	$ 869	$ 1,092	$ 1,550

Employee data:

> *To download a free copy of the Excel® file used in this scenario please go to:*
> *http://bentonexcelbooks.my-free.website/sample-data-files*
> *select the file for Chapter 5 (Employee Data) in the 'The Step-By-Step Guide To The VLOOKUP formula in Microsoft® Excel®' section.*

	A	B	C	D	E
1	SALES PERSON ID	SALES PERSON LAST	SALES PERSON FIRST	SALES REGION	MANAGER ID
2	100	Winchester	Elizabeth	West	50
3	200	Graham	Peter	West	50
4	300	Steller	Alex	Central	30
5	400	Simpson	Helen	East	40
6	500	Tanner	Joe	West	50
7	600	Graham	Maggie	Central	30
8	700	Danner	Peter	East	40

1. Insert a column on the sales report before '**SALES PERSON FIRST**'

2. Label the new **column 'A'** as 'VLOOKUP ID' *(this column is going to become our new lookup_value)*

The sales report should now look similar to the following:

	A	B	C	D	E	F
1	VLOOKUP ID	SALES PERSON FIRST	SALES PERSON LAST	Jan	Feb	Mar
2		Peter	Danner	$ 4,449	$ 7,048	$ 5,746
3		Maggie	Graham	$ 3,973	$ 6,251	$ 7,719
4		Peter	Graham	$ 1,975	$ 2,274	$ 2,719
5		Helen	Simpson	$ 7,716	$ 8,015	$ 8,460
6		Alex	Steller	$ 2,779	$ 3,002	$ 3,460
7		Joe	Tanner	$ 5,620	$ 5,843	$ 6,301
8		Elizabeth	Winchester	$ 869	$ 1,092	$ 1,550

3. In cell **'A2'** apply the following CONCATENATED formula:

=C2&" - "&B2

A2	▼ : ✕ ✓ ƒx	=C2&" - "&B2				
	A	B	C	D	E	F
1	**VLOOKUP ID**	**SALES PERSON FIRST**	**SALES PERSON LAST**	**Jan**	**Feb**	**Mar**
2	Danner - Peter	Peter	Danner	$ 4,449	$ 7,048	$ 5,746
3		Maggie	Graham	$ 3,973	$ 6,251	$ 7,719
4		Peter	Graham	$ 1,975	$ 2,274	$ 2,719
5		Helen	Simpson	$ 7,716	$ 8,015	$ 8,460
6		Alex	Steller	$ 2,779	$ 3,002	$ 3,460
7		Joe	Tanner	$ 5,620	$ 5,843	$ 6,301
8		Elizabeth	Winchester	$ 869	$ 1,092	$ 1,550

4. Copy this formula to cells **'A3' – 'A8'**

5. Insert a column between columns **'C'** & **'D'** label **'REGION'**

	A	B	C	D	E	F	G
1	**VLOOKUP ID**	**SALES PERSON FIRST**	**SALES PERSON LAST**	**REGION**	**Jan**	**Feb**	**Mar**
2	Danner - Peter	Peter	Danner		$ 4,449	$ 7,048	$ 5,746
3	Graham - Maggie	Maggie	Graham		$ 3,973	$ 6,251	$ 7,719
4	Graham - Peter	Peter	Graham		$ 1,975	$ 2,274	$ 2,719
5	Simpson - Helen	Helen	Simpson		$ 7,716	$ 8,015	$ 8,460
6	Steller - Alex	Alex	Steller		$ 2,779	$ 3,002	$ 3,460
7	Tanner - Joe	Joe	Tanner		$ 5,620	$ 5,843	$ 6,301
8	Winchester - Elizabeth	Elizabeth	Winchester		$ 869	$ 1,092	$ 1,550

6. Go to the employee data file, insert a column on the sales report before '**SALES PERSON ID**'

7. Label the new **column 'A1'** as 'VLOOKUP ID' (*this column is going to become our new **lookup_value***)

The sales report should now look similar to the following:

	A	B	C	D	E	F
1	VLOOKUP ID	SALES PERSON ID	SALES PERSON LAST	SALES PERSON FIRST	SALES REGION	MANAGER ID
2		100	Winchester	Elizabeth	West	50
3		200	Graham	Peter	West	50
4		300	Steller	Alex	Central	30
5		400	Simpson	Helen	East	40
6		500	Tanner	Joe	West	50
7		600	Graham	Maggie	Central	30
8		700	Danner	Peter	East	40

8. In cell '**A2**' apply the following CONCATENATED formula:

$$=C2\&" - "\&D2$$

A2			f_x	=C2&" - "&D2		
	A	B	C	D	E	F
1	VLOOKUP ID	SALES PERSON ID	SALES PERSON LAST	SALES PERSON FIRST	SALES REGION	MANAGER ID
2	Winchester - Elizabeth	100	Winchester	Elizabeth	West	50
3		200	Graham	Peter	West	50
4		300	Steller	Alex	Central	30
5		400	Simpson	Helen	East	40
6		500	Tanner	Joe	West	50
7		600	Graham	Maggie	Central	30
8		700	Danner	Peter	East	40

9. Copy this formula to cells '**A3**' – '**A8**'

10. If you haven't already done so, please **SAVE** both files

11. Go back to the sales report, select cell '**D2**', and apply the following VLOOKUP formula:

```
=VLOOKUP(A2,'[Employee Data.xlsx]Employee'!$A:$F,5,FALSE)
```

12. Copy this formula to cells 'D3' – 'D8'

| D2 | | | | f_x | =VLOOKUP(A2,'[Employee Data.xlsx]Employee'!$A:$F,5,FALSE) | | |

	A	B	C	D	E	F	G
1	**VLOOKUP ID**	**SALES PERSON FIRST**	**SALES PERSON LAST**	**REGION**	**Jan**	**Feb**	**Mar**
2	Danner Peter	Peter	Danner	East	$ 4,449	$ 7,048	$ 5,746
3	Graham - Maggie	Maggie	Graham	Central	$ 3,973	$ 6,251	$ 7,719
4	Graham - Peter	Peter	Graham	West	$ 1,975	$ 2,274	$ 2,719
5	Simpson - Helen	Helen	Simpson	East	$ 7,716	$ 8,015	$ 8,460
6	Steller - Alex	Alex	Steller	Central	$ 2,779	$ 3,002	$ 3,460
7	Tanner - Joe	Joe	Tanner	West	$ 5,620	$ 5,843	$ 6,301
8	Winchester - Elizabeth	Elizabeth	Winchester	West	$ 869	$ 1,092	$ 1,550

13. Highlight cells 'D2' – 'D8', COPY, and PASTE AS A VALUE the **region** information

14. After you **paste as a value**, you may delete **column 'A'** on the sales report

	A	B	C	D	E	F
1	**SALES PERSON FIRST**	**SALES PERSON LAST**	**REGION**	**Jan**	**Feb**	**Mar**
2	Peter	Danner	East	$ 4,449	$ 7,048	$ 5,746
3	Maggie	Graham	Central	$ 3,973	$ 6,251	$ 7,719
4	Peter	Graham	West	$ 1,975	$ 2,274	$ 2,719
5	Helen	Simpson	East	$ 7,716	$ 8,015	$ 8,460
6	Alex	Steller	Central	$ 2,779	$ 3,002	$ 3,460
7	Joe	Tanner	West	$ 5,620	$ 5,843	$ 6,301
8	Elizabeth	Winchester	West	$ 869	$ 1,092	$ 1,550

You now have a list of employees, their first quarter sales results, and sales region.

☑ HELPFUL INFORMATION:

While the **CONCATENATE** function is helpful when you do not have a unique **lookup_value** for your VLOOKUP formula, there are **risks** with this option. In the example above, if our data sample was larger, there would a higher probability of more than one person having the same first and last name combination. However, sometimes this can't be avoided, the risks are outweighed by the value the VLOOKUP brings to task efficiency. The next section discusses the implications of what happens when you have same **lookup_value** listed more than once.

When the unique lookup_value is listed more than once on the table_array, the VLOOKUP will always return the value for *the first* unique lookup_value it finds in the table_array. Let's walk through an example.

Using similar sample data as the above for sales and employee, we'll again lookup the employee's sales region:

Sample data *(Sales Report with two entries for the same Sales Person ID)*:

SALES REPORT:

	A	B	C	D	E
1	SALES PERSON ID	SALES PERSON FIRST	SALES PERSON LAST	REGION	Jan
2	700	Peter	Danner		$ 4,449
3	600	Maggie	Graham		$ 3,973
4	200	Peter	Graham		$ 1,975
5	400	Helen	Simpson		$ 7,716
6	300	Alex	Steller		$ 2,779
7	500	Joe	Tanner		$ 5,620
8	100	Elizabeth	Winchester		$ 869
9	300	Butler	Catherine		$ 1,588

EMPLOYEE DATA:

	A	B	C	D	E
1	SALES PERSON ID	SALES PERSON LAST	SALES PERSON FIRST	SALES REGION	MANAGER ID
2	100	Winchester	Elizabeth	West	50
3	200	Graham	Peter	West	50
4	300	Steller	Alex	Central	30
5	400	Simpson	Helen	East	40
6	500	Tanner	Joe	West	50
7	600	Graham	Maggie	Central	30
8	700	Danner	Peter	East	40
9	300	Butler	Catherine	East	40

Hopefully, there are system controls in place to prevent a sales person ID from being added more than once. However, I've seen situations where this can happen, especially when migrating data from another system or importing employee information from an acquisition.

SALES REPORT:

D6			f_x	=VLOOKUP(A6,'[Employee Data.xlsx]Employee'!$A:$E,4,FALSE)	

	A	B	C	D	E	F	G	H
1	SALES PERSON ID	SALES PERSON FIRST	SALES PERSON LAST	REGION	Jan			
2	700	Peter	Danner	East	$ 4,449			
3	600	Maggie	Graham	Central	$ 3,973			
4	200	Peter	Graham	West	$ 1,975			
5	400	Helen	Simpson	East	$ 7,716			
6	300	Alex	Steller	Central	$ 2,779			
7	500	Joe	Tanner	West	$ 5,620			
8	100	Elizabeth	Winchester	West	$ 869			
9	300	Butler	Catherine	Central	$ 1,588			

As you can see from the screenshot above, the VLOOKUP will always return the value for the first unique **lookup_value** it finds in the **table_array**.

☑ HELPFUL INFORMATION:

To address this you could apply the **CONCATENATE** function to the sales person's ID, first, and last name and make that the unique **lookup_value**. However, if you're in a position to do so, the best practice would be change the employee's sales person ID.

An easy way to identify duplicate values is use CONDITIONAL FORMATTING. For example, using the employee sample data:

1. Highlight **column 'A'**
2. From the toolbar select **HOME: Conditional Formatting**
3. From the drop-down box, select the **option 'Highlight Cells Rules'** then **'Duplicate Values...'**

EMPLOYEE DATA:

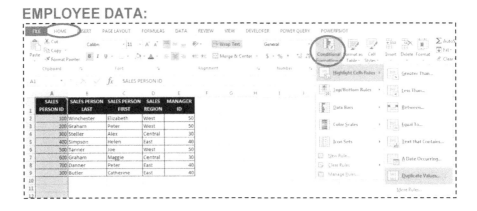

The following dialogue box should appear:

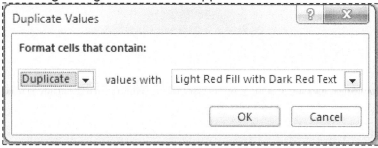

Click the '**OK**' button

The following rows should now be highlighted:

	A	B	C	D	E
1	SALES PERSON ID	SALES PERSON LAST	SALES PERSON FIRST	SALES REGION	MANAGER ID
2	100	Winchester	Elizabeth	West	50
3	200	Graham	Peter	West	50
4	300	Steller	Alex	Central	30
5	400	Simpson	Helen	East	40
6	500	Tanner	Joe	West	50
7	600	Graham	Maggie	Central	30
8	700	Danner	Peter	East	40
9	300	Butler	Catherine	East	40

To remove the Conditional Formatting:

1. From the toolbar select **HOME : Conditional Formatting**:

2. Select '**Clear Rules**' and either option:
   a. Clear Rules from <u>S</u>elect Cells
   b. Clear Rules from <u>E</u>ntire Sheet

Please see screenshot below for an example.

CHAPTER 5
APPLYING THE VLOOKUP ACROSS MULTIPLE SHEETS OR WORKBOOKS

To apply the VLOOKUP formula across multiple workbooks or sheets, we will again use the **IFERROR** function, please see chapter 4 for syntax.

Scenario:
A new sales management position has been created to oversee three sales regions. This new manager has been given a list of employee IDs, but does not know each employee's name and sales region. He has asked you to pull together all the employee data and create a consolidated report for him.

Detailed Example How To Use The Formula:

To download a free copy of the Excel® file used below, please go to: *http://bentonexcelbooks.my-free.website/sample-data-files select the file for Chapter 5 (Manager's Report)*

Sample data:
Workbook #1 (**Manager's** Report)
Manger's Report with Employee ID:

	A	B	C	D
1	EMPLOYEE ID	SALES PERSON LAST	SALES PERSON FIRST	SALES REGION
2	100			
3	200			
4	300			
5	301			
6	400			
7	500			
8	600			
9	700			
10	702			

Manager's Report ⊕

To download a free copy of the Excel® file used in this scenario please go to:
*http://bentonexcelbooks.my-free.website/sample-data-files select the file for **Chapter 5 (Employee Data)** in the **'The Step-By-Step Guide To The VLOOKUP formula in Microsoft® Excel®'** section.*

Sample data:
Workbook #2 Employee Data
Employee data contained on 3 sheets (tabs):

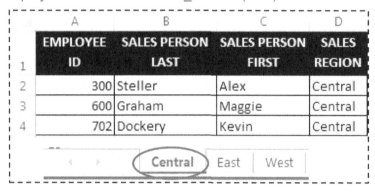

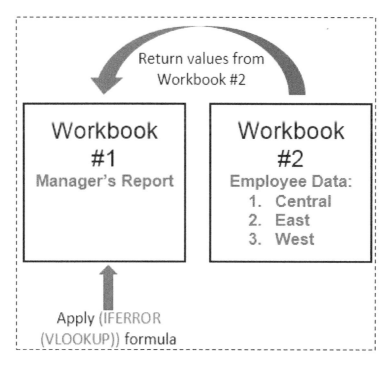

We're going to build a nested VLOOKUP formula, by the time we're done it is going be very long. However, by building step-by-step, we will minimize errors. Also, if we run into problems it will be easier to troubleshoot, because we know the previous parts we built are working.

1. Begin by going to workbook #1 (Manager's Report) and click cell **'B2'**

2. Enter the following VLOOKUP formula:

```
=VLOOKUP(A2,'[Employee Data.xlsx]Central'!$A:$D,2,FALSE)
```

You'll receive the **#N/A** message, this is _**OK**_ and to be expected.
We'll address this as we go.

Workbook #1 (Manager's Report)

	A	B	C	D	E	F	G	H
B2				=VLOOKUP(A2,'[Employee Data.xlsx]Central'!$A:$D,2,FALSE)				
1	EMPLOYEE ID	SALES PERSON LAST	SALES PERSON FIRST	SALES REGION				
2	100	#N/A						

3. Copy the above VLOOKUP formula down to cells **'B3'** – **'B10'**

Rows 4, 8, & 10 should now have values:

Workbook #1 (Manager's Report)

	A	B	C	D
1	EMPLOYEE ID	SALES PERSON LAST	SALES PERSON FIRST	SALES REGION
2	100	#N/A		
3	200	#N/A		
4	300	Steller		
5	301	#N/A		
6	400	#N/A		
7	500	#N/A		
8	600	Graham		
9	700	#N/A		
10	702	Dockery		

4. Next, we'll add the **IFERROR** function to the **VLOOKUP** formula, please go back to cell **'B2'** and enter the following:

```
=IFERROR(VLOOKUP(A2,'[Employee
Data.xlsx]Central'!$A:$D,2,FALSE),"Name Not Found")
```

5. Copy the updated IFERROR & VLOOKUP formula to cells **'B3' – 'B10'**

Workbook #1 (Manager's Report)

B2   *fx* =IFERROR(VLOOKUP(A2,'[Employee Data.xlsx]Central'!$A:$D,2,FALSE),"Name Not Found")

	A	B	C	D	E	F	G	H	I	J
1	EMPLOYEE ID	SALES PERSON LAST	SALES PERSON FIRST	SALES REGION						
2	100	Name Not Found								
3	200	Name Not Found								
4	300	Steller								
5	301	Name Not Found								
6	400	Name Not Found								
7	500	Name Not Found								
8	600	Graham								
9	700	Name Not Found								
10	702	Dockery								

Next, we'll extend the IFERROR and VLOOKUP formula, to search the *second tab* called **'East'** on Workbook #2 (Employee Data).

6. Please go back to cell **'B2'** and enter the following:

```
=IFERROR(VLOOKUP(A2,'[Employee
Data.xlsx]Central'!$A:$D,2,FALSE),IFERROR(VLOOKUP(A2,'[Emp
loyee Data.xlsx]East'!$A:$D,2,FALSE),"Name Not Found"))
```

I know the above formula is difficult to read, I've attempted highlight the section that was added for the **'East'** tab on Workbook #2. Please also note, the additional parenthesis **)** at the end of the formula.

7. Copy the updated IFERROR & VLOOKUP formula to cells **'B3' – 'B10'**

B2   *fx* =IFERROR(VLOOKUP(A2,'[Employee Data.xlsx]Central'!$A:$D,2,FALSE),IFERROR(VLOOKUP(A2,'[Employee Data.xlsx]East'!$A:$D,2,FALSE),"Name Not Found"))

	A	B	C	D	E	F	G	H	I	J	K	L	M	N	O
1	EMPLOYEE ID	SALES PERSON LAST	SALES PERSON FIRST	SALES REGION											
2	100	Name Not Found													
3	200	Name Not Found													
4	300	Steller													
5	301	Butler													
6	400	Simpson													
7	500	Name Not Found													
8	600	Graham													
9	700	Danner													
10	702	Dockery													

=IFERROR(VLOOKUP(A2,'[Employee Data.xlsx]Central'!$A:$D,2,FALSE),

IFERROR(VLOOKUP(A2,'[Employee Data.xlsx]East'!$A:$D,2,FALSE),"Name

Not Found"))

Almost done, we'll now add the final IFERROR and VLOOKUP formula, to search the *third tab* called 'West' on Workbook #2 (Employee Data).

8. Please go back to cell **'B2'** and enter the following:

```
=IFERROR(VLOOKUP(A2,'[Employee
Data.xlsx]Central'!$A:$D,2,FALSE),IFERROR(VLOOKUP(A2,'[
Employee
Data.xlsx]East'!$A:$D,2,FALSE),IFERROR(VLOOKUP(A2,'[Emp
loyee Data.xlsx]West'!$A:$D,2,FALSE),"Name Not
Found")))
```

9. Copy the updated IFERROR & VLOOKUP formula to cells **'B3' – 'B10'**

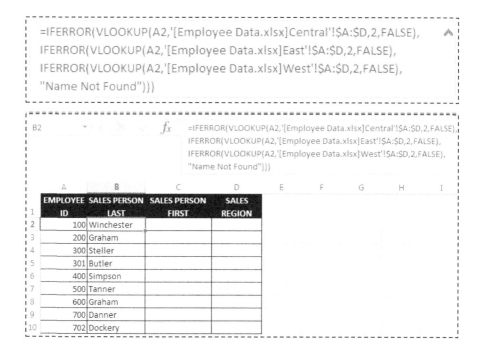

Great job! If you had trouble, don't worry, this was a complex nested IF VLOOKUP formula. You'll get better with practice. It often still takes me a couple of tries to get the formula correct and I have had years of experience. It is very easy to miss a comma or parenthesis with these advanced functions. Your skill level will improve with repetition.

To complete the scenario, we're going to copy the formula to the **'SALES PERSON FIRST'** & **'REGION'** columns on workbook #1 (Manager's Report).

10. Before we begin copying the IFERROR & VLOOKUP formula, we need to add the **dollar $** symbol to the **lookup_value**. Please see below for an example.

11. On workbook #1 (Manager's Report) click cell **'B2'**

12. For each VLOOKUP, before the lookup_value, add the $:

```
=IFERROR(VLOOKUP($A2,'[Employee
Data.xlsx]Central''!$A:$D,2,FALSE),IFERROR(VLOOKUP($A2,'
[Employee
Data.xlsx]East'!$A:$D,2,FALSE),IFERROR(VLOOKUP($A2,'[Em
ployee Data.xlsx]West'!$A:$D,2,FALSE),"Name Not
Found")))
```

B2		f_x	=IFERROR(VLOOKUP($A2,'[Employee Data.xlsx]Central'!$A:$D,2,FALSE),
			IFERROR(VLOOKUP($A2,'[Employee Data.xlsx]East'!$A:$D,2,FALSE),
			IFERROR(VLOOKUP($A2,'[Employee Data.xlsx]West'!$A:$D,2,FALSE),"Name
			Not Found")))

13. Copy the updated IFERROR & VLOOKUP formula to cell **'C2'**

14. In cell **'C2'** change the **col_index_num** for all VLOOKUP formulas to **3**

```
=IFERROR(VLOOKUP($A2,'[Employee
Data.xlsx]Central''!$A:$D,3,FALSE),IFERROR(VLOOKUP($A2
,'[Employee
Data.xlsx]East'!$A:$D,3,FALSE),IFERROR(VLOOKUP($A2,'[
Employee Data.xlsx]West'!$A:$D,3,FALSE),"Name Not
Found")))
```

=IFERROR(VLOOKUP($A2,'[Employee Data.xlsx]Central'!$A:$D,3,FALSE),
IFERROR(VLOOKUP($A2,'[Employee Data.xlsx]East'!$A:$D,3,FALSE),
IFERROR(VLOOKUP($A2,'[Employee Data.xlsx]West'!$A:$D,3,FALSE),"Name
Not Found")))

	A	B	C	D	E	F	G	H	I
C2				f_x	=IFERROR(VLOOKUP($A2,'[Employee Data.xlsx]Central'!$A:$D,3,FALSE), IFERROR(VLOOKUP($A2,'[Employee Data.xlsx]East'!$A:$D,3,FALSE), IFERROR(VLOOKUP($A2,'[Employee Data.xlsx]West'!$A:$D,3,FALSE),"Name Not Found")))				

	A	B	C	D
1	EMPLOYEE ID	SALES PERSON LAST	SALES PERSON FIRST	SALES REGION
2	100	Winchester	Elizabeth	
3	200	Graham		
4	300	Steller		
5	301	Butler		
6	400	Simpson		
7	500	Tanner		
8	600	Graham		
9	700	Danner		
10	702	Dockery		

15. Copy the updated IFERROR & VLOOKUP formula to cells
'C3' – '**D10**', please note to copy the formula to **column 'D10'**

It is OK, that **column 'D'** is displaying the same values as **column 'C'**, we'll fix this in the next steps.

	A	B	C	D
1	EMPLOYEE ID	SALES PERSON LAST	SALES PERSON FIRST	SALES REGION
2	100	Winchester	Elizabeth	Elizabeth
3	200	Graham	Peter	Peter
4	300	Steller	Alex	Alex
5	301	Butler	Catherine	Catherine
6	400	Simpson	Helen	Helen
7	500	Tanner	Joe	Joe
8	600	Graham	Maggie	Maggie
9	700	Danner	Peter	Peter
10	702	Dockery	Kevin	Kevin

16. Select cell **'D2'**

17. Change the **col_index_num** for all VLOOKUP formulas to **4**

18. Copy the updated IFERROR & VLOOKUP formula in cell **'D2'** to cells **'D3' – 'D10'**

```
=IFERROR(VLOOKUP($A2,'[Employee
Data.xlsx]Central'!$A:$D,4,FALSE),IFERROR(VLOOKUP($A2,'
[Employee
Data.xlsx]East'!$A:$D,4,FALSE),IFERROR(VLOOKUP($A2,'[Em
ployee Data.xlsx]West'!$A:$D,4,FALSE),"Name Not
Found")))
```

```
=IFERROR(VLOOKUP($A2,'[Employee Data.xlsx]Central'!$A:$D,4,FALSE),
IFERROR(VLOOKUP($A2,'[Employee Data.xlsx]East'!$A:$D,4,FALSE),
IFERROR(VLOOKUP($A2,'[Employee Data.xlsx]West'!$A:$D,4,FALSE),"Name
Not Found")))
```

| D2 | | fx | =IFERROR(VLOOKUP($A2,'[Employee Data.xlsx]Central'!$A:$D,4,FALSE), IFERROR(VLOOKUP($A2,'[Employee Data.xlsx]East'!$A:$D,4,FALSE), IFERROR(VLOOKUP($A2,'[Employee Data.xlsx]West'!$A:$D,4,FALSE),"Name Not Found"))) |

	A	B	C	D	E	F	G	H	I
1	EMPLOYEE ID	SALES PERSON LAST	SALES PERSON FIRST	SALES REGION					
2	100	Winchester	Elizabeth	West					
3	200	Graham	Peter	West					
4	300	Steller	Alex	Central					
5	301	Butler	Catherine	East					
6	400	Simpson	Helen	East					
7	500	Tanner	Joe	West					
8	600	Graham	Maggie	Central					
9	700	Danner	Peter	East					
10	702	Dockery	Kevin	Central					

The final report should look similar to the following:

	A	B	C	D
1	EMPLOYEE ID	SALES PERSON LAST	SALES PERSON FIRST	SALES REGION
2	100	Winchester	Elizabeth	West
3	200	Graham	Peter	West
4	300	Steller	Alex	Central
5	301	Butler	Catherine	East
6	400	Simpson	Helen	East
7	500	Tanner	Joe	West
8	600	Graham	Maggie	Central
9	700	Danner	Peter	East
10	702	Dockery	Kevin	Central

Congratulations! You've successfully applied a VLOOKUP formula across multiple tabs and workbooks.

You've completed the scenario, the new manager has been given a consolidated report that lists the ID, name, and sales region for all of his employees.

CHAPTER 6
VLOOKUP TROUBLESHOOTING

While the VLOOKUP and associated formulas are very useful and quite powerful, it can be challenging and sometimes frustrating to learn them. Why a VLOOKUP is not returning the correct value can puzzle even the most experienced users. The final chapter of this book addresses some of the most common VLOOKUP errors and how to resolve them. The areas reviewed are:

1. Why I am receiving the **#N/A error message**?

2. My **lookup_value** is the same as the match value in the **table_array**, why is my VLOOKUP formula not returning a value?

3. Why am I getting the **#REF error message**?

4. My VLOOKUP formula was working, but now I'm getting the wrong values, why?

ERROR / ISSUE: Why I am receiving the **#N/A error message**?

There are a number of reasons why you'll get the #N/A error message, but the most likely cause, especially for beginners is:

- The field you want to match, the **lookup_value**, <u>IS NOT</u> the <u>FIRST COLUMN</u> in the range of cells you specify in the **table_array**.

Let's take a closer look, in the example below, the VLOOKUP formula is fine, but since we're matching on the 'SALES PERSON ID', this column needs to be FIRST in the table_array.

SHEET 1:

| A2 | | f_x | =VLOOKUP(B2,Sheet2!A:C,2,FALSE) |

	A	B	C	D	E	F
1	SALES PERSON NAME	SALES PERSON ID	Jan	Feb	Mar	
2	#N/A	200	$ 869	$ 1,092	$ 1,550	

SHEET 2 (table_array):

	A	B	C
1	SALES PERSON NAME	SALES PERSON ID	REGION
2	Graham, Peter	200	West
3	Steller, Alex	1174	Central
4	Simpson, Helen	500	East
5	Tanner, Joe	833	West

Solution: Make the 'SALES PERSON ID', the first column in the table_array.

SHEET 2 (table_array):

	A	B	C
1	SALES PERSON ID	SALES PERSON NAME	REGION
2	200	Graham, Peter	West
3	1174	Steller, Alex	Central
4	500	Simpson, Helen	East
5	833	Tanner, Joe	West

SHEET 1:

A2	▼	⋮	✕	✓	*fx*	=VLOOKUP(B2,Sheet2!A:C,2,FALSE)

	A	B	C	D	E	F
1	SALES PERSON NAME	SALES PERSON ID	Jan	Feb	Mar	
2	Graham, Peter	200	$ 869	$ 1,092	$ 1,550	

ERROR / ISSUE: Why I am getting the **#N/A error message**? My **lookup_value** IS the FIRST COLUMN in the range of cells specified in the table_array. What else could be wrong?

The next two examples can be a little more tricky to understand as they involve formatting issues, such as *extra spaces* and/or mismatched *case* of the lookup_value.

Let's first review the issue of extra spaces in the lookup_value or table_array. When I first started using VLOOKUP formulas, I was having trouble getting one to work. I literally spent hours trying to figure out why it wasn't working. After banging my head against my desk, I realized there were extra spaces in my lookup_value. Most of the time you can't see extra spaces, especially if they are after the lookup_value, but these invisible nuisances will cause your VLOOKUP to fail. Below is an example:

- Can you see the **extra spaces** in the below screenshot?

SHEET 1:

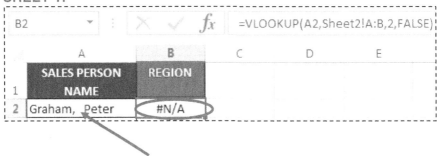

B2	▼	⋮	✕	✓	*fx*	=VLOOKUP(A2,Sheet2!A:B,2,FALSE)

	A	B	C	D	E
1	SALES PERSON NAME	REGION			
2	Graham, Peter	#N/A			

Solution: First identify where the extra spaces are and then remove them.

To identify where the extra spaces are, I use the **LEN** formula. The **LEN** formula *counts the number characters* in a cell. In the below example we can see that:

- In **sheet 1** for the lookup_value, the LEN formula is indicating more characters compared to what is contained in the table_array. The names:
  - Graham, Peter should only be 13 characters
  - Simpson, Helen should only be 14 characters

Although I can't easily see these extra spaces (characters), they exist and are causing my VLOOKUP to fail.

SHEET 1:

	A	B	C
1	SALES PERSON NAME	REGION	LEN
2	Graham, Peter	#N/A	15
3	Simpson, Helen	#N/A	16

SHEET 2 (table_array):

	A	B	C
1	SALES PERSON NAME	REGION	LEN
2	Graham, Peter	West	13
3	Simpson, Helen	East	14

Now that I know where the problem is, I will remove these extra spaces by using the **TRIM** formula. The **TRIM** formula *removes all extraneous spaces* from a cell, except for single spaces between words.

SHEET 1:

	A	B	C	D
	SALES PERSON NAME	REGION	LEN	TRIM
1				
2	Graham, Peter	#N/A	15	Graham, Peter
3	Simpson, Helen	#N/A	16	Simpson, Helen

D2 | | | | | | =TRIM(A2)

Next, I will **paste as a value** the results of the TRIM formula into **column 'A'** and this will fix the VLOOKUP error.

SHEET 1:

	A	B	C
	SALES PERSON NAME	REGION	LEN
1			
2	Graham, Peter	West	13
3	Simpson, Helen	East	14

If you would like to learn more about **LEN** & **TRIM** formulas, please check out my book:

The Step-By-Step Guide To

The 25 Most Common Microsoft Excel Formulas & Features

ERROR / ISSUE: Why else would I be getting the **#N/A error message**?

A similar formatting issue that will cause a VLOOKUP to fail is related to mis-matched *case* of the lookup_value.

Below is an example:

- The last name of GRAHAM, Peter is all **uppercase**
- The entire name of simpson, helen is **lowercase**

SHEET 1:

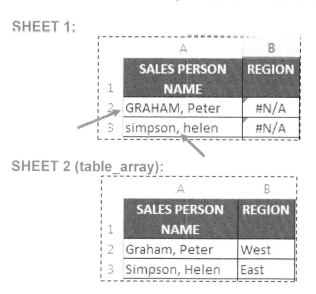

SHEET 2 (table_array):

	A	B
	SALES PERSON NAME	REGION
1		
2	Graham, Peter	West
3	Simpson, Helen	East

Solution: Use a text function to make the case formatting consistent with the table_array.

In the below example, I will use the formula **PROPER** to change the lookup_value. You may also use formulas **UPPER** or **LOWER** if you choose:

SHEET 1:

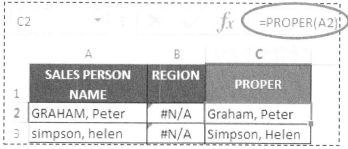

Next, I will **paste as a value** the results of the **PROPER** formula into **column 'A'** and this will fix the VLOOKUP error.

SHEET 1:

B2	▼	⋮	✕	✓	*fx*	=VLOOKUP(A2,Sheet2!A:B,2,FALSE)

	A	B	C	D	E
1	SALES PERSON NAME	REGION	PROPER		
2	Graham, Peter	West	Graham, Peter		
3	Simpson, Helen	East	Simpson, Helen		

ERROR / ISSUE: Why am I getting the **#REF** error message?

Like the **#N/A** error message, there are a number of reasons why you'll get the **#REF error message,** but one of the more common causes is:

- The **table_array** range of cells is incorrect.

In the example below, the VLOOKUP in sheet 1 is referencing *2 columns* in the table_array. The **#REF error** is because the **col_index_num** is referencing *column 3*, but that column is NOT included in the table_array.

Please see below screenshots:

SHEET 1:

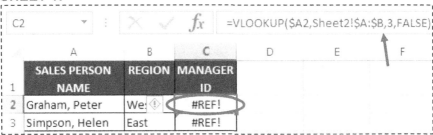

C2	▼	⋮	✕	✓	*fx*	=VLOOKUP($A2,Sheet2!$A:$B,3,FALSE)

	A	B	C	D	E	F
1	SALES PERSON NAME	REGION	MANAGER ID			
2	Graham, Peter	We⊙	#REF!			
3	Simpson, Helen	East	#REF!			

SHEET 2 (table_array):

	A	B	C
1		Number of Columns:	
2	**1**	**2**	**3**
3	**SALES PERSON NAME**	**REGION**	**MANAGER ID**
4	Graham, Peter	West	50
5	Simpson, Helen	East	40

Solution: Change the table_array to include the correct number of columns.

SHEET 1:

C2			f_x	=VLOOKUP($A2,Sheet2!$A:$C,3,FALSE)

	A	B	C	D	E	F
1	**SALES PERSON NAME**	**REGION**	**MANAGER ID**			
2	Graham, Peter	West	50			
3	Simpson, Helen	East	40			

ERROR / ISSUE: My VLOOKUP formula was working, but now I'm getting the wrong values, why?

Again, there can be a number of reasons why a VLOOKUP will suddenly stop working, but one of the more common causes is:

- Someone has inadvertently added or deleted columns in the **table_array** range of cells.

In the example below, REGION *was* being populated correctly. Let's say, you reviewed this report on a Friday, but then on the following Monday, when you opened the same report, the results were different. Why?

SHEET 1 (correct on Friday):

	A	B	C
1	SALES PERSON NAME	REGION	MANAGER ID
2	Graham, Peter	West	50
3	Simpson, Helen	East	40

SHEET 1 (incorrect on Monday):

	A	B	C
1	SALES PERSON NAME	REGION	MANAGER ID
2	Graham, Peter	100	West
3	Simpson, Helen	200	East

After reviewing the table_array, you discover someone has added **two new columns**; 'SALES PERSON ID' and 'HOME OFFICE LOCATION'.

SHEET 2 (table_array)

	A	B	C	D	E
1	SALES PERSON NAME	SALES PERSON ID	HOME OFFICE LOCATION	REGION	MANAGER ID
2	Graham, Peter	100	Seattle	West	50
3	Simpson, Helen	200	London	East	40

Solution: Adjust your VLOOKUP formula to account for the newly inserted columns.

SHEET 1

B2					f_x	=VLOOKUP($A2,Sheet2!$A:$E,4,FALSE)

	A	B	C	D	E	F
1	SALES PERSON NAME	REGION	MANAGER ID			
2	Graham, Peter	West	50			
3	Simpson, Helen	East	40			

Thank you!

Thank you for purchasing and reading this book, I hope you found it helpful! Your feedback is valued and appreciated! Please take a few minutes and leave a review.

OTHER BOOKS AVAILABLE BY THIS AUTHOR:

1. The Step-By-Step Guide To The **25 Most Common** Microsoft® Excel® Formulas & Features

2. The Step-By-Step Guide To **Pivot Tables** & Introduction To **Dashboards**

3. The Microsoft® Excel® **Step-By-Step** Training Guide **Book Bundle**

Made in the USA
Las Vegas, NV
31 July 2023